TRUE BIGFOOT STORIES:

Eyewitness Accounts of Killer Bigfoot Encounters:

Terrifying Stories of Sasquatch Creatures

By

Max Mason Hunter

LIKE FREE BOOKS?

Would you like them delivered to you every week?

Do you like non-fiction books on a huge range of different topics?

We send out FREE e-books every week so we can share our books with the world!

We have FREE books every week on AMAZON that we send to our email list.

So if you want in, then visit the link at the end of this book to sign up and sit back and wait for new books to be sent straight to your inbox!

TABLE OF CONTENTS

Introduction

Chapter 1

The Legacy Of Patterson And Gimlin.....................................1

Chapter 2

Bigfoots – Man Killers?..4

Chapter 3

Roosevelt, Beavers And Death.............................6

Chapter 4

Old Legends Of Bigfoots...10

Chapter 5

Someone Or Something – Bigfoot 911 Call...........................14

Chapter 6

Marble Mountain – Entering Bigfoot Territory....................16

Chapter 7

Nevada – Searching For A Yeti..18

Chapter 8

The Winnemucca Encounter – Face To Face With The Beast..21

Chapter 9

Cannibal Giants Of The Jarbidge Forest..............................23

Chapter 10

Cold War Bases Of Finland – Bigfoot Events Surrounding Them...32

Chapter 11

Kusta's Cabin And Unwanted Visitors.......................................40

Conclusion

INTRODUCTION

There are many things you need to worry about when wondering the woods. Getting lost, attacked by bears, wolves, snakes and so on. But let's not forget about one of the most popular creatures that roam the woods all across the world, Bigfoots.

But Bigfoots aren't real, you might say. They're just a myth, a story, a scam, a hoax, a publicity stunt. All of those things and more have been said on the subject...

And yet, for decades now, scientists all over the world have spent millions, in both cash and man-hours, investigating this phenomenon. Why would they do this? Why spend time and money on a myth? Why dedicate your life to a practical joke? Because that's what it must be, right?

And all of those videos and sightings of them? Just products of imagination and attempts to cash in on the gag, of course. People encountering Bigfoots is nothing uncommon, stories like that have been around for thousands of years.

Are all of them really lies though? Out of the thousands of these stories, are we really meant to believe none of them are true? We could say all of those people are liars, but sometimes, you just can't ignore the numbers you're dealing with.

So if you do believe it's just a myth and a joke, why should you keep them in mind when roaming the woods? Because the most dangerous thing is the one you're not expecting...

CHAPTER 1

THE LEGACY OF PATTERSON AND GIMLIN

Where the Bigfoot myth caught 'fire' the most is America. To this day, the Sasquatch believers are mostly living in the United States, with the rest of the world a bit behind on the matter, even though stories and the mystery surrounding the humanoid creature have reached far beyond the small towns where they first began.

So what of the encounter that kick started the whole phenomenon? This one is something that most people are familiar with, the infamous Patterson-Gimlin footage. If that doesn't ring a bell, its description should.

It's 1967. The location is the woods in California, near Orleans. Two friends were horseback riding when they spotted a strange creature. It was hairy, peacefully doing something with its hands, crouched down behind some foliage.

They both halted their horses and observed it, hoping it hadn't spotted them. Patterson was very excited by the sight, but so was his horse. It was alarmed by the creature's presence. Patterson managed to calm his horse after a bit, after which he got off and took out his camera...

"Cover me", he said to Gimlin, as he ran towards the creature, which started moving away from them, into the woods. As he got closer to it, Patterson noticed it's size. He claimed it was around seven feet tall, which is a bit over two meters.

Sputtering, he aimed his camera at the creature, forever cementing the moment in history. In the short video, which is about a minute long, the creature can be seen walking away from them, and at one point, it turns its body sideways and looks directly at the camera.

This moment of basic motion has been the discussion of scientists and many others since it was first shown. Surprisingly, most of the scientists actually say that the footage is not fake. And these aren't self-proclaimed scientists either, but people who are well educated, grounded and do research for a living.

Would these people really risk their reputation and jobs by saying something that ridiculous if they didn't actually believe it? Scientists live and breathe off their ability to be objective, and present information in the most bold and unbiased way possible. If so many of them were willing to call it real, who are we to disagree?

Unsurprisingly, many people did, claiming that the footage is a fake and just a successful publicity stunt. What is shocking though, is that the number of people who say its real are much higher in number, and these people, as I mentioned, are serious scientists and researchers.

But what happened after the famous video ended? After the creature disappeared into the woods? Gimlin, who jumped off his horse the second his friend asked him to cover him, got back on his horse and then followed the creature as it roamed the woods.

After following it for a while, he lost sight of it. While Gimlin followed it, Patterson used what remained of his film to record the creature's footprints. He would have joined his friend, but his horse ran off, probably out of fear.

His friend also wasn't there to cover him anymore, and his rifle was back on his horse. He felt unnerved in that position, scared that the creature's mate might show up.

Luckily for Patterson, nothing of the sort happened. The only thing coming out of the woods to get him was his friend. He told him he lost the creature to the woods and then escorted his friend back to his horse.

After Patterson saddled up himself, they searched for the Bigfoot, using their tracking skills. But their tracking skills couldn't do much when the track led into terrain which made it impossible to tell where the creature went.

So what of the duo after everything was over? Patterson passed away due to cancer in 1972, sticking with his statement that the video was not a hoax, just like Gimlin, who's still alive. He never talked of the encounter much, but has been active on Bigfoot gatherings since the famous incident.

One of the most notable things he said is that before the encounter, he doubted the existence of Sasquatches, and that it completely changed his mind. It's 2016, a different century and to this day nobody has been able to prove the recording is fake.

That is the burning question isn't it? Some people have spent decades researching Bigfoots without calling their existence a hoax. Can it be that these creatures actually exist, that they roam forests all over the world, observing us, without us even knowing how close we are to the mythical creature? But the why of it is what's interesting.

If we assume that Yeti's/Sasquatches/Forest People/Bigfoots really do exist, that opens up a whole new book worth of questions. Why do they exist? Which species are they? Are they more ape or man? How can they keep their existence so secretive, even from people who actively search for them? And, most importantly, what do they want with us?

Are they hostile or friendly? If hungry, would they hunt us? Would they consume our flesh? Would they kill to defend their territory? One thing we know for sure is that a lot of people go missing in the woods, never to be seen again…

CHAPTER 2

BIGFOOTS – MAN KILLERS?

America, being the place where Bigfoot sightings happen most often, is logically the place where the most serious of Bigfoot believers are. There are a lot of these groups and many of them are quite active. They hold gatherings, discussions, go on trips, in short, everything Bigfoot related. A huge amount of these people also find calling Bigfoots 'Man-killers' is insulting and plain wrong.

They say that Bigfoots aren't aggressive, and point out that, if that was the case, we wouldn't be seeing any Bigfoot sightings at all, since logically, a giant Bigfoot could easily kill any man if that was his goal. One of the stories, that of a man called Matthew Johnson, supports this claim.

His first encounter with the creatures happened on the first of July, year 2000. He was out in the Oregon woods with his family when he spotted it. The huge, hairy creature was right in front of him, in plain sight.

He was scared for both himself and his family, as he had no means to protect them. The Bigfoot eventually went away, but the event and its impact changed his life forever. He had nightmares about it for years, and wasn't comfortable sleeping in a forest for long after the incident.

But that's not where his story ended. Matthew didn't just have this encounter and move on, actually, the absolute opposite is true. Today, he runs a website dedicated to everything Bigfoot related, where he writes blogs, sells products, his books and shares his findings with the world.

He has equipment set up in the woods which he uses to record all night, hoping to catch any Bigfoots making noise. He's made numerous comments on the creatures, and refers to them as Forest People. He considers that to be the proper name for them.

Matthew fully agrees with people who claim that Bigfoots are not violent creatures. He said, in one of his blogs, that if it were true, he wouldn't be sharing his story. This is a pretty good point, but one that brings up more questions.

Yeti's might not be violent on sight, but what if they have a reason? If someone enters their territory, or if they feel threatened? What would a Yeti do then? Would he flee, escaping from conflict? Or would he take more drastic measures to defend himself?

This important bit of questioning is something Matthew has addressed in his blogs. He said that it makes sense that a Yeti would attack to defend his territory and safety, but that you shouldn't feel like your life is in danger. You should just accept you're not welcome and that you should move outside its territory.

That's a reasonable point. If a giant hairy beast shows aggression, moving away does sound like a good idea. But there is one part of this conundrum that he missed. What if you're not able to move away?

What if you're cornered in a cave? What if you're tired and can't outrun him? What if you fall? What happens when you end up at a dead end and have to face the force of nature head on?

If a Yeti would show aggression to defend his home, would he act upon it? One man found out just that, and it was the last thing he'd ever learn...

CHAPTER 3

ROOSEVELT, BEAVERS AND DEATH

Not all Bigfoot stories showed up after the infamous Patterson-Gimlin recording. Actually, some of the first stories that include creatures which descriptions match those of Bigfoots, go all the way back to Native Americans, and their stories of giants taking people away at night deep into the woods, never to be seen or heard from again.

But the story I'm focusing on here is not one that is as old as that. This one dates back to before the 1950's, years before Bigfoots became a cultural phenomenon. The term Bigfoot was a lot less used back then and was something mostly known by hunters and trappers alike.

Besides the time period, there is another detail that makes this story special. It was told by none other than Teddy Roosevelt, one of America's presidents. Now the encounter wasn't actually his, he just retold the story of a trapper called Bauman who shared it with him.

Even though Roosevelt couldn't add anything to the story itself, as he wasn't there, he could say plenty about Bauman's demeanor as he shared it with him. Teddy said the man couldn't help but shiver at certain parts of it and that he was obviously still shaken by the things he saw and by what happened to his friend, even though years had passed.

Bauman was trapping in Beaverhead County-Montana with a friend when it happened. Their aim was to find a suitable location to camp near good trap spots.

They rode far and deep into the woods on their mountain ponies, as far as they could, but they eventually had to go on foot, as the terrain wasn't safe for horses. They set out on foot, and after a few hours, they found what seemed to be the perfect location for a camp. They set up camp haphazardly, hoping to set up at least a few traps before nightfall, as it was late already.

The business of setting up traps went as expected, no interruptions and nothing out of the ordinary. But when they went back to their camp, things were different.

It was ravaged. Their stuff was throw around and claw marks on some of them. Both men thought of this as nothing but an inconvenience.

Bears weren't uncommon in Beaverhead County. They didn't have time to panic or complain, as the night was nearing. They restored their camp the best they could and then went to sleep...

Bauman's friend took some time to examine the tracks the creature left, curious of its whereabouts. He paced back and forth, eventually informing Bauman that the bear walked on two legs. Bauman laughed at the comment, thinking his partner was joking. He made it clear he wasn't, telling Bauman to see for himself.

Since it was already dark, they lit a torch and looked over the tracks again, together. Bauman ended up agreeing with his friend, that the creature was bipedal, but after toying with the idea that a human ruined their camp, they elected it couldn't have been human tracks.

They both went to bed, but their night was not easy, as a disgusting, sharp smell snapped Bauman out of his slumber. He spotted a dark, giant figure watching the camp...

It made a terrible noise, maybe due to being spotted. Bauman didn't waste a second, he grabbed his rifle and fired at the figure.

He missed, and the creature, whatever it was, ran inside the forest. Its screams, as Bauman described them were devilish. They were both up now and unnerved by what just happened so they stayed up until morning. But there was nothing but silence all night.

You might think they both got out of there the second the sun came up, but they didn't see it that way. They were both young and adventurous, but weren't stupid enough to think everything was entirely normal. They spent the entire day close to each other, with an eerie feeling they were being watched.

Soon, darkness would come to the forest again. A new fire was needed and this time, one of them would keep watch while the other slept.

The Bigfoot did show its face again, but it had learned. It didn't come close to their camp, it just observed from a safe distance and yelled in anger. They could hear twigs breaking in the distance. It was agitated.

Bauman hoped it wasn't due to hunger...

After a long night of hearing otherworldly howls, it was time for them to check up on the final set of their traps and then leave. Their final day there was quite good. The weather was perfect and warm, and they didn't feel like they were being watched anymore.

They actually relaxed and joked about the situation. Then came the time to leave and head back to civilization. Relaxed or not, they weren't leaving each other's side. Not until the final moments.

Bauman said he would go get the rest of the traps, while his partner packed everything up. This would not be the last time Bauman saw his friend, but it was the last time he saw him alive. Bauman was at the traps, happy with what they caught. He got distracted for a bit, only noticing when the sun started going down.

He packed up quickly and headed back to camp. It was in his sights now, he could see the fizzled out fire and their stuff neatly packed, ready to go. He shouted his friends name, but got no reply.

Soon, he was close enough to see what gruesome fate was bestowed upon his friend. Bauman ran up to his friends laying body. His neck was broken, with teeth marks all over it. He was dead, and it was recent. The body was still warm. And right next to him were the exact same tracks as the ones they found before...

Bauman panicked. He knew he had to make his way back right away. He left his friends body, all the gear, everything except for his weapon, then walked without stopping until he reached the ponies. He rode off to safety.

The story does sound unbelievable, but let's not forget which man decided it was worth sharing in a serious tone. Roosevelt himself, a man who never wasted his time joking around or spreading rumors. If he shared Bauman's tale without even a touch of sarcasm, it's a story worth looking into.

What this encounter tells us, if real, is that Bigfoots are not only capable of murder, but of quick learning. The way he didn't come close the second night and only attacked when one of them was alone, shows impressive intelligence. But the way the man was killed is what's the biggest point of interest, not only because of the way he was killed, but also why.

The creature snuck up on him, bit down on his neck then broke it. The fact the Bigfoot was capable of stealth is very frightening, but more so, is the why of the killing. Why did it act in such an extreme manner? Was it due to Bauman's aggressive demeanor the first night?

Or was the creature even aiming to kill? What makes the most sense is that they made the camp too close to the Bigfoot's territory, making it uncomfortable. It's scary, but not completely out of the question to think that the Bigfoot they encountered on each day was a different one.

It might have been a territorial killing, as it didn't take or eat the body. If its aim was his flesh, Bauman wouldn't have found anything at all. One thing's for sure, always have company when in the woods...

CHAPTER 4

OLD LEGENDS OF BIGFOOTS

As I mentioned before, tales of hairy, tall and violent humanoids living in the woods have been around since the days of Native Americans. None of their stories name any of the monsters mentioned as Bigfoots, but the description of them match what we would generally consider to be one.

Time muddles many things, making it impossible to tell if some of these stories are actually true or simple folklore tales.

The Expedition

This story follows a man called Joshua LeFlore and a group of Native Americans who joined him on his mission of finding missing children in Oklahoma. The exact year this search took place is hard to pin point, the best assumption one could make is that it took place somewhere between the early 1800's and early 1900's.

The area which LeFlore and his search party covered was the Choctaw territory, where most of the events took place. If they knew Bigfoots were behind the deed or if they at least suspected it, is something that's not entirely clear.

All the men did come fully armed and loaded, so even if they didn't suspect Sasquatch's, they were expecting trouble. The number of missing cases wasn't small either, it being somewhere in the twenties.

LeFlore and his gang found the children, but not in a state they'd hoped for. Their bodies were all piled up on top of one another, forming a small hill in the woods. Soon after their find, a pack of hairy giants started rushing towards them.

The Bigfoots intent was obvious, so they all opened fire. LeFlore was in the front, leading the group and was the first one to fall. One of the Yeti's swung its claws at his horse, killing it. LeFlore emptied all of his bullets into the creature, but it wasn't enough to take it down. The Yeti swung its claws again, killing LeFlore on the spot.

The rest of the search party was equipped with rifles. They fired at the Bigfoots, all of them aiming for the head, which seemed to be the only way to take the creatures down reliably. After they killed two of them, the rest of the Bigfoots retreated back to the woods.

The Natives let them go, except for the one that killed LeFlore. They hunted that one down, killed it and then chopped its head off. They then buried what was left of the children's bodies and LeFlore, after which they burned the dead bodies of the Sasquatches, before riding home...

The Headless Valley

Another Yeti related story was given life in a similar time period, but in a completely different country. The Nahanni Park in Canada is a place shrouded in death and mystery that haunt it till this day.

Many people call the park the Headless Valley, due to its history. The earliest occurrence of gruesome events that earned it that name, date back to 1906. A priest found a lone, severely sick man by the river. He helped him recover, and when the man could, he told him about the events leading up to his rescue.

The man wasn't in the park alone, but with a friend. They were camping together, when out of nowhere, in the middle of the night, a group of huge hairy creatures attacked them. They focused on his friend, dragging him into the woods, tearing him apart, gutting him and biting his flesh.

After they finished eating, they tore off his friend's head and took it with them. The surviving man was sick when the priest found him due to exertion. He didn't stop to eat, drink, sleep or think about what he was doing. He was too petrified to do any of that. He just ran.

But this story alone isn't what earned the Headless Valley its title. There were more cases, similar to this one. One took place a mere two years after the first one. A pair of Macleod brothers set their sights on the Nahanni Park. Their goal was digging gold, as it was a popular area for that at the time.

A year passed since they left, with no word from them to their parents or anyone else. Their corpses were soon found by the river. Their heads, missing. Several cases matching these were recorded over the years.

In 1917, another gold digger tried his luck in Nahanni, Martin Jorgenson. Martin spent a good bit of time scouting the valley, trying to find the best spot to set up his mining operation. He had everything set up, even building a cabin to live in.

Later on, his cabin burned to the ground with him in it. After the flames fizzled out and his remains were recovered, it seemed as though his head was missing to. The head was never found...

In 1945, a miner from Ohio suffered a similar fate. He was found dead in his sleeping bag with his head removed.

Those are only a few of many gruesome mysteries that shroud the beautiful park. The biggest question is, are Yeti's behind the headless killings?

It could have been a Native tribe behind it all, some people suggested. Experts looked into the matter and concluded that the tribes being behind it all is unlikely, as all tribes in that area ceased to exist before the first recorded incident.

Even though it's beautiful, much of the Nahanni Park actually remains unexplored. Whoever is behind the numerous beheadings that took place there, might be there, deep inside the Headless Valley.

The Native's Folklore

Bigfoot-like creatures played a big part in the Native Americans folklore. They were depicted as angry, cannibalistic humanoids. The stories tell a great deal about them, most of them depicting them as evil.

They were said to kidnap children to eat and take young woman for breeding. The stories say they would carry out the kidnappings at night, sneaking into camps, finding their victim and then dragging them with them into the forest.

Compared to the modern depictions of Bigfoots, which is as peaceful, generally non-violent creatures, this is a huge contrast. But it also points to something very interesting. Bigfoots, in almost all stories featuring them, seem to possess human like intelligence.

What might have happened is that humans developed such effective ways of defending ourselves from them, that they stopped seeing us as an easy prey. Not only does this match up with the data, but it would also prove that Bigfoots aren't just a wild, brainless beast pushed along by pure instinct.

It would show that they're more akin to us than they are to wild animals. Which makes them all the more terrifying to think about...

CHAPTER 5

SOMEONE OR SOMETHING – BIGFOOT 911 CALL

Police stations receive a lot of strange calls, many of which are just pranks. The Washington State Police Department received a call that seemed to be just that, on one night in 1990.

The dispatcher answered the call. The first thing she asked was the usual – "911. What are you reporting?" But what the man replied with wasn't something very usual.

"We got someone or something, crawling around here..." – he replied. She asked if it was an animal. He replied that he wasn't sure and that he only saw it for a split second before it vanished into the darkness. His outside sensor light came on, which was the reason why he noticing anything in the first place.

In his next sentence, he said it might be a huge man in his backyard, or something similar to that. The dispatcher asked him if there were any other recent problems in the area. He said that his dog was killed a few days before, and that whatever did it was standing on two legs.

The creature ran off too quickly for him to catch it that day. He went on to say that he couldn't see anything outside of the window anymore and that he didn't want to leave his house. Before he got to finish his sentence, he started screaming, sounding shocked and scared.

The dispatcher said – "Hello? What's going on now sir?" The caller said the creature was in plain sight again, and that he was looking straight at it. He said he looked almost seven feet tall, and that he was completely covered in dark hairs...

The dispatcher asked him – "But it is a person, right?" – with nervousness in her voice. The man took a while and said yes, hesitating. In the end he said that it might have been just a very big person, and that they should send someone over.

Soon, the police were there, but they were late. The creature was already long gone. A few weeks later, in the same area, someone reported seeing a Bigfoot in their backyard.

They also managed to take a picture of it. Nothing more came of these two sightings though, they were both slowly forgotten about...

CHAPTER 6

MARBLE MOUNTAIN – ENTERING BIGFOOT TERRITORY

Another famous piece of footage capturing what might be a Sasquatch was recorded by Jim Mills, who was leading a group of special needs students while they wondered the Marble Mountain Wilderness in California in 2001. The video starts with Jim recording a student messing around in an odd structure they found.

The structure resembled a small hut, obviously meant to keep someone or something safe. They messed around with it a bit more, without a care, until one of the students pointed out a strange figure in the distance. Jim, who was already recording, aimed the camera right at the mysterious figure.

It was far away from them, but its figure and movements were clear. To this day, this recording remains one of the most talked about recordings of Bigfoot, mostly due to its high quality compared to most.

It also shows something that's quite rare, a Sasquatch like creature moving around in the open, with its motions clear. The first of what can be seen of the creature on the video, is it slowly going down the hill.

Its legs and arms seemed abnormal and far too long to be a human. It walked down until it reached two trees, where it stopped and looked at the group of students. Besides standing around, the Bigfoot also screamed in their direction, possibly angered that someone was on its territory.

It didn't rush towards them though, it mostly stayed around the same area, getting more aggressive with its movements every minute. It tore off some braches and jumped around in anger for a while.

After that, it appeared to have calmed down, and kept on going down the hill. Some of the people nervously joked around, saying – "It's gonna be real funny when the guy comes down here to say hi." – and similar comments.

Right before it disappeared behind the mountain, one of the students suggested they should try and shoot it to finally prove Bigfoot exists.

Jim said they're definitely not going to shoot him. The student then went on to say they could tranquilize it, but before he finished his sentence, the video cuts to the next day. Jim is standing in the same spot as yesterday, and while filming the environment, says they hadn't seen the Bigfoot since he disappeared behind the mountain yesterday.

What's your opinion on this...? Was the sighting real?

CHAPTER 7

NEVADA – SEARCHING FOR A YETI

Many of the Bigfoot fan clubs go on what they call "Bigfoot hunting" trips. Now although it might sound that way, the point of these expeditions is not to find and kill a Bigfoot. Most, if not all Bigfoot fans consider them to be misunderstood, peaceful creatures.

Their goal is to merely experience seeing a Bigfoot in person, with their own eyes. These Bigfoot hunts are organized by numerous groups around the world, most of which are in America.

The year in which the one I'm talking about in this segment took place in 2000, in Nevada. A group of Yeti enthusiasts, about twenty of them or so, were spending time in the wild, hoping to finally experience meeting a Yeti. A good chunk of this group were sceptics and newcomers, both of which are very common on Yeti hunts.

"The intrigue of seeing a Yeti is quite strong, even if you think they're just a fairy tale." – said one of the people after the incident. This expedition was a bit unusual from the start. Instead of going deep into the woods as usual, their leader decided they should stay close to the road.

The decision was made due to the number of inexperienced people in the group. He feared he wouldn't be able to keep an eye on everybody. The decision wasn't received well by most, but it stayed.

It took them a few hours to set up a camp near the road, and when they were just about done, the night was very close. A campfire was made and then the wait started. One of the things that the guides guaranteed would happen is that they would hear Bigfoots in the night...

The road being close wasn't an issue, as cars passed by very rarely, the forest was more silent than usual that night and no Bigfoot-like noises were heard. The people would have walked away disappointed, if not for what happened next.

One of the campers walked further outside the camp, near the road. When later asked why, he said he didn't like hearing all the Bigfoot stories the people in the group were sharing, as he found them absurd.

His opinion would soon change...

He was standing right next to the road, in almost complete darkness. He heard a car get closer. He looked in its direction. He saw its bright, blinding headlights before he saw the car.

He fixated his eyes on the car, following it. The car was fast, but in the moment it passed right in front of him, thanks to its headlights illuminating the nearby forest, he spotted a dark, hairy figure with long arms and legs just on the other side of the road for a split second. He only saw it for a flash, but it was convincing enough that he ran back to camp in a hurry.

The other campers described his demeanour when he was back at the campfire as, 'shaken to his bones'. He shared what he saw with the others. Some laughed, some were scared, but they were all curious.

They were all going to see if his story was true for themselves. While they all gathered to move, the head of the group said any lights should remain off, as to not alert the creature to their presence.

Walking at a hurried pace, they could soon see where the scared man was standing when he spotted the hairy beast. What they could also see was the spot where the Yeti was. The scared man whispered – "There..." – and pointed at the spot with his finger.

They didn't move any further, not just out of fear of the creature, but also out of fear they'd scare it off. The group silently watched over the spot for a good few minutes, until they saw movement. Some leaves and bushes were moving on their own...

Some campers got scared and started yelling, which is what possibly scared off the Yeti. Before the trees and bushes stopped moving, they saw what the scared man saw for a brief second.

A hairy, tall creature with long arms and legs...

The story was later covered by several TV stations, before it was forgotten about...

Was this for real? What did they see?

CHAPTER 8

THE WINNEMUCCA ENCOUNTER – FACE TO FACE WITH THE BEAST

It was 2005 when a 6-year-old boy went to visit Winnemucca in Nevada with his uncle and older cousin. Their story takes place in February, meaning cold weather and deep snow.

The snow was much deeper than it was in the years before. Also with them was their uncle's dog. The uncle's dog wasn't easily scared, as he fought a mountain lion a few years before but he was heavily scared after the fight.

The uncle parked the vehicle where people usually would when they hiked in that area but he noticed there were no other cars parked there except for his. The uncle let his dog loose, who ran up the mountain ahead of them right away.

They hiked for a while, when the boy screamed – "There's a man up there!" – pointing up the mountain.

The other two looked up, but no one was where the boy was pointing. They both figured the kid was messing around with them, as nobody else could be there except for them. It made no sense, not just because their car was the only one there, but also due to tracks.

They didn't see any recent tracks in the snow leading up. They were the only ones making them. After some more hiking, something unexpected happened. The uncle's dog ran back to them, whimpering and scared.

It hid behind its owner. Never had the animal acted in such a manner before, making the uncle worried. They all stopped. The cousin asked his uncle if he wanted to head back or keep going. Before his uncle responded, he had something bigger to worry about...

The kid was right. There was someone up there with them, but it was no man. A Sasquatch was standing on top of the hill they were climbing. It wasn't moving at first, it just made disgusting and strange sounds. They were aggressive and very low pitch.

None of them moved, out of shock and fear. A few minutes passed before the creature started moving towards them. It was slow, but it wasn't stopping. It kept making the same disturbing sounds as it moved.

It slowly dawned on the uncle that he was facing a Sasquatch in the flesh. He quickly realized they needed to get back to their car right away. The little boy was picked up by his cousin, who took one final glance at the creature, before he started running down the mountain.

They all got out of there safely. None of them shared their story with anyone, not until 2014, when the cousin shared it with a member of a Bigfoot club, Terry. He said he never shared the story with anyone, as he thought people would call him crazy or a liar.

The story was spread online later that year, when Terry visited the area of Winnemucca where the event took place, and recorded a video of himself sharing it...

CHAPTER 9

CANNIBAL GIANTS OF THE JARBIDGE FOREST

The Jarbidge forest is located in Northern Nevada, but it wasn't always called that. The Natives called the area Tsawhawbitts mountains, but that's not the only difference. The Indians would never dare venture even close to the area, as they believed Bigfoot-like creatures lived there.

They also said these creatures were cannibals and man-eaters, who would kidnap anyone who came close. Today, the Jarbidge forest is a very popular area for hunting and camping activities.

Our story takes place in August of 2014, when a hunter and his step-father set foot in Jarbidge in hope of hunting deer.

The story was shared by the young man, who never shared his real name, nor his step-fathers. The only person he calls by their name in the whole story is Mike, who shows up later down the line. For convenience sake, I'll call the story-teller Jack for the rest of the tale.

Jack shared his story with an ambitious group of Bigfoot believers that go by the name of RMSO (short for Rocky Mountain Sasquatch Organization).

They didn't have a planned amount of days to stay there, Jack just said they were going to stay until they had had enough. He also talks a great deal about the weather conditions they were faced with, even before they got there.

The rains were heavy, long and happened throughout their whole stay there. Some parts of the country were flooded, while everything was muddy, making tracking difficult. This wasn't Jack's first time visiting the area, but it was his step-dads, who was excited to see what the area had to offer.

They drove there with a trailer, which was attached to Jack's truck. One of the more intriguing parts about Jack is that this was not his first experience with Yeti's, but he never went into more detail about that first experience...

Even though he had a previous experience with Bigfoots, he was still a sceptic before what happened to him in Jarbidge. He mentioned he always carried a flashlight and his weapon at all times when he was in the woods because of his first encounter, and that what happened in Jarbidge transformed him into a complete believer of Bigfoots.

This was going to be the third concurrent year that Jack would be using this camp location. They got there close to nightfall, so they set up camp quick, so they could at least scout a little before they lost vision.

Jack ran into something that intrigued him while he scouted the area around the camp. A broken tree. It looked as though it was snapped by brute force, which didn't make much sense to Jack. He knew what kind of a tree it was and how tough they are to break.

He called for his step-dad to join him. The tree was broken at an almost perfect ninety-degree angle, pointing at the camp. Jack suggested they should try doing the same on a similar tree before night comes.

They easily found one and tried, but no luck. They simply didn't have enough strength between the two of them to snap it like the one they found. They had no time to think about what might have done it, as night was upon them.

They made their way back to camp. His step-dad fell asleep with no issues, but Jack didn't feel comfortable enough to close his eyes and sleep. He said it was too quiet, which unnerved him. He had stayed in the same area before, and it was never completely silent at night, which was exactly what it was on this one.

He remembered the rule he made for himself after his first Bigfoot encounter, which was to have his weapon and flashlight close at all times. He had neither at that moment, they were both in his truck. He got up and went to get them...

While he was getting the truck door open, the weather started to worsen. Periodic flashes of lighting started happening. When one of them flashed, Jack spotted a giant, hairy creature which was very close to the truck. It didn't seem to Jack like it was walking towards him, but to the right.

He panicked, opening the trucks door as quickly as he could, then getting his Glock and flashlight. He used the latter to light the area where the creature flashed in front of him for a second, but he saw nothing.

Feeling less scared, now that he was armed, he went on to check for tracks. As he suspected, the creature was moving to the right, with the tracks obviously showing it. They soon became too muddled and deformed to be differentiated from the tracks his step-dad and him were making.

Jack moved back to the trailer, thinking whether or not he should share what happened with his step-dad or not. He went back into his side of the tent and tried to relax for the night. As he drifted asleep, something snapped him out of it. He could hear someone walk on the mud close by, right outside his tent...

He got out of his sleeping bag, grabbed his Glock and looked in the direction the sounds were coming from. He could see the tent move, as the creature touched it. Jack saw the shape of its hand as it moved it around...

What scared him the most was that the sounds of someone stepping on mud were still far from his tent, meaning there was more than one creature close by. Soon after, he heard the creatures outside breaking and throwing their stuff around. Soon after, they started throwing small rocks at the tent.

This terrified him. If there were two or three, there could be more. He had thirteen bullets in his glock, but he didn't fire, even when he had a clear shot on one of them. His reasoning was that he didn't want to risk making the Bigfoots angry, as the number that was surrounding them wasn't clear.

He had plenty of ammunition, but shooting blindly into the darkness seemed like a bad idea. He had another reason for not opening fire, which was his step-dad, he was an incredibly heavy sleeper, and was still sleeping while everything was taking place.

Jack didn't want to risk his step-dad's life. Opening fire would certainly wake him up and leave him an easy target for the Sasquatch's, as he wouldn't know what was going on. Jack tried waking him up by whispering his name a few times, but it didn't work. He didn't dare scream to wake him, thinking it would rouse the Bigfoots even more.

He also wasn't sure if his weapon would be powerful enough to take down even one Bigfoot. Jack was trying to wake his step-dad up when he heard a loud noise, that sounded like water falling down a rain gutter at a high speed.

He then realized that one of the Bigfoots was urinating right next to the tent. It didn't sound like regular human urinating, it sounded much stronger, like a giant animal was doing it. Hearing it made Jack even more scared. At this point he said he reached a panic level so high that any reason he had shattered.

He grabbed the nearest thing to him, which just happened to be made of aluminum, and threw it at his sleeping step-dad while screaming at him to wake up. He did hit his step-dad with the object, but not before it bounced off one of the metallic parts of the tent, making a loud noise...

The noise scared the Yeti that was urinating, who then made a noise Jack couldn't find words to describe, before running away from the tent. His step-dad was finally awake, grumpy that Jack hit him with something. Jack quickly informed him of what was going on for the last few hours. Not believing a word of it, his step-dad walked outside the tent...

Jack thought such a move to be absolutely insane, but he didn't let his step-dad go alone. Both of them were outside now, watching over their camp. The campfire they made earlier was destroyed, while everything else was thrown around.

Tracks were everywhere, some were good, but most bad, due to mud. There were so many of them that neither of the men could tell how many creatures were surrounding them just a few seconds ago. The only thing that they could take away from the tracks, is that they were big.

It would be a while before they got out of there, as all the mud made for a difficult road. Jack's step-dad was fully focused on driving out of there, while Jack was scouting around for any more Bigfoots.

He spotted none. After a long few minutes of tension and fear, they were finally out of there. Now that they were on the road, Jack's step-dad decided to drive to the nearest town.

Jack talked about his feeling after the event, describing them as the most intense feelings of fear he had ever felt in his entire life. His step-dad was awake for only a few minutes, while Jack endured more than an hour of psychological draining at the hands of a supposed myth.

His step-dad noticed Jack was still holding his glock. He didn't like the way he was holding it, and worried for him, he asked Jack to give it to him. Jack refused, as he still didn't feel safe or calm enough to drop his weapon. In the end, his step-dad convinced him to at least un-chamber the round.

While they drove to town, Jack looked at his watch for the time. He almost didn't believe it, but only a bit over an hour had passed since he was awoken from sleep by the Bigfoot. To him, it had felt like he was there for several hours.

They made their way to the town. Jack didn't share anything much about that part, the only thing he said was that they decided they had to go back to get their stuff as soon as possible. They waited for the sun to be high up before going back.

They didn't bother sharing their story with anyone in town nor did they call any authorities over the incident. Like it seems to be the case in many Sasquatch encounters, it usually takes some time and the right person for people to open up about them.

When the weather got nicer, they drove back to their camp. They expected to find it completely wrecked and destroyed, but were surprised to find it in the same condition as before. This indicates the Bigfoots interest was purely in the humans that were there, not their food or anything else.

Jack and his step-dad didn't see anything driving there either. They both felt much safer with the sun being so high up, but they knew they couldn't stay there long. They packed things up as quickly as they could, aiming to be out of there in just a few minutes...

They sadly ran into a huge progress halter, which was the trailer itself. The part of it that gets attached to the truck was stuck and unusable without fixing it. Luckily for them, fixing it in this situation meant hitting it with the strongest thing they had to snap it in place.

Jack grabbed a hammer and went to work. He was certain Bigfoots would hear him hit the hook, no matter how gently he'd do it, so instead of trying to keep quiet, he bashed it as strong as he could.

He bashed it a few times before he noticed something in the corner of his eye… He turned to his left and saw a Bigfoot. It was just standing there, in the open, calm, watching him. Jack then mentioned how every animal knows that staying like that in the open is a death sentence and that none would do it unintentionally.

Jack turned to his step-dad and yelled – "Bigfoot there!" – and when he turned his head back to where the Bigfoot was, it was already running into the depths of the forest. His step-dad didn't turn in time to see it in the open, but he did see it for a second or two, before it disappeared.

Jack also talked about the creature's height, which he wasn't sure about. Even when it was fully exposed and in front of him, he couldn't tell for certain, due to its pose which made it seem like it was slouching or crouching down a bit.

Even when it was running away, he couldn't tell, as the creature remained in a similar, bent down pose. Another thing it did before it vanished was make a noise similar to the one Jack heard the night before, one that he didn't have words to describe.

Jack went back to tinkering with the mechanism. After a few more hits, it got unstuck and was ready to be used. His step-dad moved the car to the spot and Jack attached the trailer. They went on their way, hoping Bigfoots wouldn't show their faces again. They didn't, but Jack and his step-dad weren't leaving the Jarbidge and its horrors just yet.

Instead of leaving, they decided to stay and give hunting deer another try. It's not clear whose idea it was, but the decision was made to switch to a safer, more often used camp location.

This is where they met Mike. Jack described Mike as an elderly gentlemen and a friend. They shared what happened last night with him. Mike was the only person Jack shared his first Bigfoot experience with, which made Mike doubt he was telling the truth this time.

"What? Again?" – said Mike after hearing their story. He first brushed it off as nothing but a joke, but he soon noticed both Jack and his step-dad were dead serious. But it took until the night came for Mike to be fully convinced. The first night they stayed in Jarbidge wouldn't be the only one in which they encountered Bigfoots...

This time, they heard a terrifying noise coming from the forest, same as the one from before. It scared all of them, as they all knew the details of yesterday's encounter well. Jack expected another pack of Sasquatch's to show up, but nothing of the sort happened the first night.

Jack asked his step-dad and Mike to listen closely to the Bigfoot making noise. He wanted them to try and distinguish if there was more than one screaming at once. The screams didn't last long, with none of the men noticing any overlapping in the noise.

The screams might have gone away, but Jack's fear hadn't. The other two also seemed frightened to him. None of them slept easily that night and they took shifts keeping watch until the sun went up.

It is at this point when Jack mentioned the length of their stay, which was twelve days total. He said the events of the remaining days meshed all together in his head, as most nights were identical.

Horrifying noises from one Sasquatch and occasional sounds of someone walking around just outside of the camp. One moment that Jack remembered clearly happened when he was checking the area around the camp with his flashlight with Mike joining him.

Mike spotted a pair of what he described as green, huge eyes staring at him. He pointed at them and screamed to Jack to light that area, but before Jack got there, he could already hear the creature run off into the darkness, breaking branches and stepping into mud.

The last thing Jack remembered was the moment when the lone Bigfoot entered their camp and started bumping into things. The loud noises woke both Jack and Mike up. Jack felt confident that this Yeti was alone and that he wouldn't be hard to take on...

He grabbed his gun and walked outside, swearing and screaming at the creature. The Yeti got frightened, starting to run away. Mike joined Jack in his swearing at the monster.

When it disappeared into the forest again, the creature broke a tree in half. Its sound was so loud that it woke Jack's step-dad up, who thought Jack and Mike were shooting their guns, as the sound of the tree breaking was that strong.

The next day they went and checked on it quickly. They found the broken tree and inspected it, it didn't seem like it was broken by accident, as immense strength would be needed to break it in such a manner.

The only conclusion they could reach is that the Bigfoot broke it out of anger. The other nights were all very similar and uneventful. As I mentioned before, Jack shared his story with the RMSO, around twenty or so months after the incident.

The RMSO was inspired by his story, and decided to search the area of Jarbidge. Equipped with high tech gear, they ventured into the forest, looking for any signs of Bigfoots. Their expedition was lengthy, but sadly yielded no Bigfoot sightings.

They did however find more than a few Bigfoot-like tracks and plenty of trees that were broken in half...

CHAPTER 10

COLD WAR BASES OF FINLAND – BIGFOOT EVENTS SURROUNDING THEM

America isn't the only place that's rich with Bigfoot folklore and stories. Yes, it might be the biggest place for it and the most popular stories are from America, but that doesn't mean other places in the world don't have any Bigfoot encounters.

Scandinavian countries, as an example, have incredibly rich Bigfoot folklore, and many tales, both fictional and real ones. Almost every Scandinavian country has its own names and beliefs about Bigfoots, and the one I'm focusing on, as it relates to this story, are ones found in Finland.

Peikko is what they call Bigfoots, although that can also be translated as Wildman. They believe there are two types of them, Vuorenpeikko and Metsänpeikko. Vuorenpeikko Bigfoots live in the mountains, while the other kind live in forests.

There are stories of both friendly and aggressive Bigfoots there. They say that the aggressive ones kidnap people and eat them, while the friendly kind will leave you alone, as long as you stay respectful to the forest and its habitants.

The deeper you go inside the forest, or higher up a mountain, your chances of meeting them increase. For this chapter, I'm covering a two-part story that takes place in Finland, which starts with a group of friends exploring its woods.

Part 1

The story was shared by one of the members of the group, who started off by saying where they were. The group was near the Porttipahta Reservoir, which is located in the upper Northern part of Finland. The year was 2009.

They decided to hike to an abandoned Cold War era military facility, which only took them around two days of hiking. He said the trip was great at first, that hiking to it was easy and that they spent a lot of time shooting random objects and exploring the base.

They spent their first couple of nights there inside one of the bases abandoned warehouses. Later on, they moved out and set up their camp outside of the base and cooked stew. Everything seemed normal, until they heard a loud and disturbing roar coming from the woods...

They were all terrified and grabbed their rifles, then stared into the darkness, scanning it for the creature that made the awful sound. The man telling the story said he could see something move, around hundred meters outside of their camp.

He could hear it move around the camp for a while, until it ran inside one of the military structures. After it entered, everything went dead silent. There were no more roars or footstep noises, just the sound of their stew boiling on the fire.

They relaxed a bit and talked about it. In the end, they laughed at themselves for getting so scared of some bear. In the morning, while they were packing, one of the men spotted someone standing on top of the biggest facility in the base.

It was too far away for anyone to see what it was. The man who told the story started searching his bag for his binoculars, to get a better look. Before he even took them out, his friends screamed that the creature was moving.

The man looked back at the facility, which the creature left by running down on one of its walls and then disappeared behind one of the buildings. It was now clear to all of them that this creature was not just a human in a suit messing with them.

They all packed quickly and started leaving the base, they were terrified, even though it was broad daylight. The group didn't stop moving until nightfall, they decided that the best idea was to always have someone on guard duty.

The man who shared the story was the first one on duty, lasting from one to three o'clock in the morning. Everything seemed peaceful to him at first. Local birds were making noise, which was normal. At one point, a lone rabbit went inside the camp and walked around.

All of a sudden, the animals started acting odd. The man noticed it right away. The birds stopped making any noise and the rabbit, who was calm a minute ago, seemed tense.

He stopped moving and stood straight up, like he was listening to something. He then started running away from the camp. This worried the man greatly, so he took out his flashlight and scanned the area with it.

Even though the flashlight wasn't particularly strong, it still helped him spot movement in the woods. There was someone there, but it was too far away to see clearly. His rifle had a scope, so he used it to zoom in on the area.

He first saw a pair of yellow eyes looking at him. The creature then stood up. The man said it was at least seven feet tall and that its hair, which covered its entire body minus the face, was dark. The creatures face was much brighter than the other parts, but the man couldn't describe it with words.

"It just had a face." – he said. The man had absolutely no idea of what the creature was or what it wanted, but he was sure of one thing. That it wasn't human. He dropped his flashlight and gripped his rifle...

He opened fire, holding the trigger down until he ran out of ammunition. He couldn't see the creature anymore, as he'd dropped his flashlight, so he just fired blindly in its general direction, hoping to hit it.

The fire woke up his friends right away, who started screaming in confusion and fear. He emptied his magazine and once again, the forest was quiet, he picked the flashlight up again and aimed it at the forest.

The creature was still there, on the same spot. After standing calmly for a few seconds, it dropped to the ground and started slithering towards them, making strange noises. They all started screaming in fear, picking up their weapons and things in a hurry, before running away.

It seemed to the storyteller that they ran around ten kilometers before taking a break. They were all shaking, none of them saying a word. After they rested for a bit, they walked their way to a public camping area where their car was parked.

They met some German tourists who were grilling sausages next to their trailer. The storyteller said the sight of other people made him feel safe and happy, but he didn't say a word to any of them. He remembered their shock when they saw them enter the camp with guns in their hands, ready to fire.

They got to their car and drove out of there as fast as they could and discussed everything. They all agreed that, whatever the creature was, it was neither fully human or animal.

This is the point where most Bigfoot stories would end, but not this one. The group, trying to show how tough and brave they are, decided to go back to the old facility a year later, and find out what exactly the creature was...

The second time they went there, they were ready for anything. They brought a camera, a vehicle that drove better on rough terrain if they needed to escape, better weapons and an extra person, making the group size, four people.

Things seemed normal when they returned at first, with birds singing and no signs of Bigfoots anywhere. They decided to map the area and make sure that they checked every single corner of the base then they made a camp in the old warehouse they had used before.

They slept in shifts again. The first night, just like the day, was uneventful. The next day they started exploring the area outside of the base and found something that looked like a bird's nest, only it was giant and made out of tiny trees, which seemed to be cracked, not cut.

Inside of the makeshift nest-like structure was a rotting moose carcass and many kinds of animal bones. The sight made them uneasy. They made their way back to base carefully. They parked their vehicle closer to the warehouse when they got there. Once they went back inside and got to their camp, pretty much everything was destroyed.

The expensive cameras they brought were smashed against the ground and destroyed, along with almost everything else. They started taking anything salvageable into their ride, then drove out of there as fast as they could...once again...

They reached the public camp area, where a policeman stopped them. He asked to see their gun permits and then asked if they were interesting in helping him with something. Apparently, a person went missing in the area, the officer said that their vehicle would make the search much easier.

They all quickly looked at each other and shook their heads, one of them said that he was late and then they drove off. Sometime later, they found out that the missing person was found dead. The man who shared the story was too scared to look up any details about the missing case, but the one thing he was sure of is that he would never go camping there again...

Although this is the end to their Bigfoot story, this is not the end to the whole thing. Let's look into the missing person case in more detail.

Part 2

The man who went missing was an immigrant from Thailand, his reason for being in the forest were business related, he was a berry picker. Many people in Finland make money this way.

This type of job is very common for people who have a hard time finding any serious work, and it's quite simple. You get assigned a location to cover and an amount of berries to collect. After you're done, you call a person and let them know they should pick you up at the designated location.

This is exactly how it went for this man, but something was a bit strange since the start. When he called the driver to pick him up at the spot, he said he was near it but also added that an animal was following him around, but that he wasn't sure which species it was.

"Near" is the word to look out for here. He never said he was right there on the spot. When the driver got there he found no one. The man wasn't waiting for him and he didn't seem to be anywhere close. He tried calling his number but he got no reply.

Later that day, the police got involved and so did the other berry pickers from the area. They formed a search party and covered the whole forest. Eventually, the man's body was found.

He was dead.

His body was wounded, it had scratches, scars and bite wounds all over it. His body was found not so far from the meeting point, which was the first thing that made no sense, when you take into account all the other aspects.

First off, the wild life in the area was incredibly passive and people-shy. Even the more aggressive predators stay away from humans. After forensics looked over the body, they concluded that his wounds weren't the cause of death.

Another thing they considered was that he died from hunger or thirst. That might seem like the end to his tale, but it wasn't. After his body was found and examined, a member of the Finish military stepped forward to make a statement about the situation.

He said that they were deeply involved in it since the moment they heard of the case, and that they helped the local police and berry pickers to find the missing man. He also said that they spoke with the missing man over the phone at one point.

He said the missing berry picker sounded panicked and that he was saying something or someone was following him. If any case raises any eyebrow, it's this one. From the start things don't make a lot of sense...

For one, the military never gets involved in missing person cases as they have no reason to. But for this one, they went out of their way to help. Another thing, of course, is the death and the state the man was found in.

He wasn't eaten, far from it. His body was in one piece when he was found, with some minor wounds on him. This doesn't seem to be a killing out of hunger by an animal, but a territorial one instead.

The Bigfoot in this area seems to show territorial behavior, which is more than obvious in the first part of the story. Another thing is where the body was. It wasn't far from the meeting spot, which doesn't add up.

When the man called the driver he said he was close to the pickup spot back then, but, when the military talked with him he said he was running away from something. What could have happened is that the creature started aggressively hunting him after his call, which got him lost.

After killing him, the Yeti might have dragged his corpse where he'd been found, which was one of the more popular theories.

Whatever we call the mysterious hairy creature that haunts the Cold War base near Porttipahta Reservoir, one thing's for certain. They might not want to eat us, but that won't stop them from killing us...

CHAPTER 11

KUSTA'S CABIN AND UNWANTED VISITORS

This story is another one outside of America, this one taking place in Estonia in the 90's. It's about a man called Kusta, who had a rough divorce and wanted to spend some time alone with his thoughts.

He owned a cabin near the city of Rakvere, but didn't live in that city. Kusta mentioned that he didn't buy the cabin, that it was his fathers and was passed on. He didn't use it often, but it was the best place to run away from his problems at that moment.

Kusta had to make a small trek to the cabin, which was nothing special. It was a very small and simple cabin, meant to be used as a safe location to rest when hunting and nothing more. Kusta planned to stay a few days and hunt goose.

He brought his shotgun with him, plentiful ammunition and many tools, along with some food. He didn't take that much food, as he planned to cook some of the goose to eat but he brought all the tools needed for it.

When he finally reached his father's cabin, he noticed something was off right away. He hadn't visited it in years, but he didn't expect this. The front door was smashed in, broken off the hinges and laying on the floor inside the cabin. He noted the door was a good few feet away from the door frame.

The front door wasn't made of light wood, so it would take a considerable force to break it in that far. He carefully entered the cabin. It only took him a minute to search the whole place. As he expected, he found no one inside.

What he did find however, was a cabin that was smashed but not robbed. He found it incredibly odd and confusing, why someone would break into a place to then not steal anything valuable.

Someone did walk in, that was obvious, as some chairs and tables were flipped over. But the drawers didn't seem to be opened and nothing was missing. He checked each drawer and to his surprise, there was some money in one of them, which he forgot to take with him when he was there the last time.

And yet, it wasn't taken and neither was anything else. He felt confused, but happy, as he found some money. He miscalculated on how long the hike there would take him, as it was almost night already so he quickly fixed the cabin up and took out one of the cans of beans he brought to eat.

He put it on the table and then tried to reattach the door. The nights there wouldn't be warm, so fixing it was a priority. As he was doing so, he saw something in the corner of his eye...

He turned his head quick, but whatever his eyes caught wasn't there anymore. He wasn't even sure if it was anything, so he wrote it off as his imagination the first time. After trying for a while, he had to deal with the fact he would be sleeping in a cabin with no door.

He didn't have the tools to fix it or the skill to use brute force to put it back on the hinges. So he did the best he could and put the door over the entrance, then went on to eat his supper, threw some coal in the fireplace, poured his beans onto a plate and warmed them up and made a quick call with his cell phone to a repairshop about his door.

The fireplace was keeping the place around it relatively warm, but anything further was too cold for him and he couldn't get comfortable enough to sleep anywhere else in the cabin.

He took one of the chairs and put it in front of the fireplace, covered himself in a blanket and closed his eyes, trying to sleep, he wasn't sure how much time passed before a loud noise woke him up.

He looked to where it was coming from, the front door. He thought he heard a knocking noise. He stood up and slowly walked up to the nearby window, still covered in his blanket. He couldn't see anyone outside. He looked through the window for a few minutes before going back to sleep.

Once again he wrote it off as nothing but his imagination going wild and went back to sleep.

His plan was to start hunting goose. The sun was up and he was ready to hunt. He grabbed his weapon and went on his way. He moved the door out of the way and walked out, the cold air hit his face, waking him up a bit more.

He walked the area around the cabin, looking up, hoping to find some goose to shoot. Soon enough, he spotted a couple, but they were on the ground. He wasn't sure why they weren't in the air, they were an easy target.

He aimed and fired, taking one down, the rest flew away. He ran up to his target excited, feeling a rush he hadn't felt in ages, he reached it and picked it up, satisfied with himself. He was getting ready to move on, when he noticed something strange...

He picked up some movement in the corner of his eye again. He turned, but unlike before, he actually saw something. A dark, tall figure was on the hill above. He only saw it for a split second, but he was sure that he saw something.

He didn't know what it was, but it was there. He wasn't disturbed or scared by the events so far. Everything seemed pretty normal to him, just a little inconvenient. On his way back to the cabin, he remembered the state he found the cabin in.

He wondered again, who did that to his cabin and what their reason was, he considered the possibility that it was just a crazy person doing it for no reason, but thinking about it scared him, so he went with another explanation.

That it was just some animal who did it. He kept looking behind himself, as he felt like someone was there. He didn't hear or see anyone, it was just a feeling he had.

Like eyes were pointed at him. It freaked him out enough to make him speed up his walk back to the cabin. When he was close to it, another feeling crept in. That something was waiting for him at the cabin, or that something had trashed it again.

He soon reached the cabin, which seemed to be in the same exact shape as he left it in. He took another look behind himself, then walked inside and put the door back the way it was.

He felt more relaxed at this point, but also hungry. Kusta was a terrible cook and he knew that his goose meal would be a disgusting failure, but he felt happy that he was doing something on his own. He was fully absorbed during the whole process, not even noticing that night was nearing.

While he was busy mixing his boiling goose stew with a wooden spoon, he heard a loud noise coming from the outside. It was a sharp, quick and demonic noise, as he put it. He stopped doing everything. He looked at the door and went for his shotgun, he grabbed it, held it close to his chest and stared at the door.

He heard steps right outside of it. They then stopped for a second then started again. It was moving towards the window, whatever it was. Kusta was terrified and ready to fire, then the creature showed its head at the window...

"You called?" – the creature said. Kusta put down his shotgun feeling stupid. It was the repairman. Kusta went to the door and moved it out of his way. He apologized for being so tense, then explained he heard some strange noise outside.

The repairman said he also heard something strange, but that it was probably just some animal. Kusta asked him why he came so late. The man said he didn't have any time to fix Kusta's door that day, as his schedule was full, but that he felt his situation was urgent enough to drop by while going home.

Kusta thanked the man and told him he owed him a drink. The man jokingly replied he'd settle for some of his goose stew. The man said that to fix the door would take about an hour so, Kusta, touched by the repairman's kindness, walked out of the cabin with his shotgun, telling him he'd catch him a goose to take home.

Kusta walked around a bit but found nothing. He didn't want to give up, so he headed a bit further, after some more walking, he did find an animal. But this one was already dead, it was a carcass of a bear.

It didn't look fresh and wasn't fully eaten, the sight confused him greatly. The area he was in wasn't known for having that many bears in it, yet alone animals that could do this to one. He tried thinking about it harder, but the disgusting smell of the bears carcass overpowered his senses.

Stepping away out of disgust, he heard the same sharp noise he heard before. It seemed to be coming from his cabins direction. He started running towards it as fast as he could. When he reached it, he found no one there, the repairman was gone and his door wasn't fixed.

Actually, the door was on the ground, like someone just dropped it there. Kusta heard the noise again. It was to his right, coming from the hill, he turned and saw the same, dark figure again.

Only this time, it wasn't hiding, it was tall, with long arms and hair everywhere. Kusta was too afraid to just stand there and look at the creature. He left everything behind and started running down the hill to his car.

He drove home right away and called the same repair shop the next day. He was genuinely surprised when the same man answered the phone. Kusta asked him what happened yesterday. The man said he saw a hairy, tall creature looking at him over the hill...

The repairman froze in place, but after it started making noise, he didn't waste a second getting out of there. Kusta then shared his part of the story. They both laughed it off and called each other babies, even though they both knew something wasn't right in those hills...

What would you have done?

CONCLUSION

What can be said about the elusive Yeti creature that hasn't been said a million times already? The stories and the folklore behind it live on, for thousands of years. But not in the usual way.

Most people aren't aware of Native American's folklore about them, or the stories. And yet, those same people, who are fully ignorant of such tales, experience these tense and life changing events every day.

The legacy of the Bigfoot is not the Bigfoot itself. We can call Bigfoot a Sasquatch, a Forest person, a Yeti, a Peikko, and it wouldn't matter. No matter what you call the creature, its descriptions are always pretty much the same.

It's tall, it's hairy, it's scary, it's mysterious, strong and intelligent and we just can't seem to catch it. Maybe the idea behind the Bigfoot lived on for so long due to our own nature. Maybe it's just a reflection of our own insecurities as creatures.

Our fear but fascination with the unknown. With something that's always one step ahead of us. Something that we will never fully understand. Something that will always confuse us, and leave us wanting. Something that will make us scared of nature, of things outside of our control...

The Bigfoot, real or not, is very real in one place. Our minds...

If you enjoyed this book, do you think you could leave me a review on Amazon? Just search for this title and my name on Amazon to find it. Thank you so much, it is very much appreciated!

OTHER BOOKS WRITTEN BY ME

Below you'll find some of my other popular books that are popular on Amazon and Kindle as well. You can visit my author page on Amazon to see other work done by me. (Max Mason Hunter).

Unexplained Phenomena

Unexplained Phenomena – Book 2

Bizarre True Stories

True Paranormal

True Paranormal – Book 2

True Paranormal – Book 3

True Ghost Stories And Hauntings

True Ghost Stories And Hauntings – Book 2

True Ghost Stories And Hauntings – Book 3

True Paranormal Hauntings

True Paranormal Hauntings – Book 2

True Paranormal Hauntings – Book 3

True Paranormal Hauntings – Book 4

Ghost Stories

LIBRARY BUGS BOOKS

Like FREE books?

Would you like them delivered to you every week?

Do you like non-fiction books on a huge range of different topics?

We send out FREE e-books every week so we can share our books with the world!

We have FREE books every week on AMAZON that we send to our email list. If you want in, then visit the link below to sign up and sit back and wait for new books to be sent straight to your inbox!

It couldn't be simpler!

www.LibraryBugs.com

If you want FREE books delivered straight to your inbox, then visit the link above and soon you'll be receiving a great list of FREE e-books every week!

Enjoy :)

MAX MASON HUNTER

Hi, I'm Max Mason Hunter, here's a bit about me;

I'm an author, self development fanatic and I have a huge amount of passion and interest for the paranormal, conspiracy and ghost stories of our worlds history!

I love to delve into our worlds most intriguing hauntings, paranormal accounts and true ghost stories that have left science scratching their heads. There has been so many unclear and bizarre happenings that have been recorded that make us all wonder: What else is out there that we don't know about?

With my books I intend to bring you the most interesting, unusual and bizarre ghost stories, paranormal hauntings and unexplained phenomena.

I hope you enjoy them as much as I enjoy writing them!

Max Mason Hunter

37680434R00035

Printed in Great Britain
by Amazon